THE AWESOME INNER WORKINGS OF VIDEO GAMES

ARIE KAPLAN

Lerner Publications Company • Minneapolis

NOTE TO READERS: Not all games are appropriate for players of all ages. Remember to follow video game rating systems and the advice of a parent or guardian when deciding which games to play.

Lerner Publications Company
A division of Lerner Publishing Group, Inc.
241 First Avenue North
Minneapolis, MN 55401 U.S.A.

Website address: www.lernerbooks.com

Content Consultant: Crystle Martin, postdoctoral researcher, Digital Media and Learning Hub at the University of California, Irvine

Library of Congress Cataloging-in-Publication Data

Kaplan, Arie.
    The awesome inner workings of video games / by Arie Kaplan.
        pages   cm. — (Shockzone — games and gamers)
    Includes index.
    ISBN 978–1–4677–1250–7 (lib. bdg. : alk. paper)
    ISBN 978–1–4677–1779–3 (eBook)
    1. Video games—Design—Juvenile literature. I. Title.
 GV1469.3.K34 2014
 794.8—dc23   2013001160

Manufactured in the United States of America
1 – MG – 7/15/13

TABLE OF CONTENTS

Under the Hood 4

The Brains of the Operation 6

A Software Kernel That Really Pops! 8

Writing in Code 10

Revving Up the Game Engine 12

Where Games Live 14

A Great Memory 18

From Console to TV 20

Pushing the Game's Buttons 22

Tapped Out 24

A Player in Motion 26

Breakthroughs in Game Technology 28

Further Information 30

Index 31

UNDER THE HOOD

You love playing on the latest video game console, but have you ever taken a moment to think about **what's going on inside that mysterious box?** Ever wonder what goes through all of those cords? Or how Mario knows to jump when you hit the A button? Turns out, the answers to these questions are totally interesting. Even better, they're not as tough to understand as you might think.

console =
a device used to
play video games

Gamers buy millions of video game consoles each year. Ever wonder how those small boxes make your favorite games possible?

SONY.

PLAYSTATION 3

Blu-ray Disc

60GB

Believe it or not, whether you're using an Atari 2600 from the 1970s or a PlayStation 3, most game systems are basically the same. Sure, the graphics look better on more modern consoles, and the ways of controlling games have changed. But the same kinds of parts are found inside just about all of them. Pretty much every console has the following guts:

- Processors
- Software kernel
- Computer code
- Storage space

- Memory
- Outputs
- Controls

All of these parts work together to bring your games to life. But what does each part do, and how do they play nice together to bring games to your TV screen? Let's crack open the plastic and dive inside a game console to figure out how all the pieces work.

Surprisingly, the same kinds of parts are inside these two consoles.

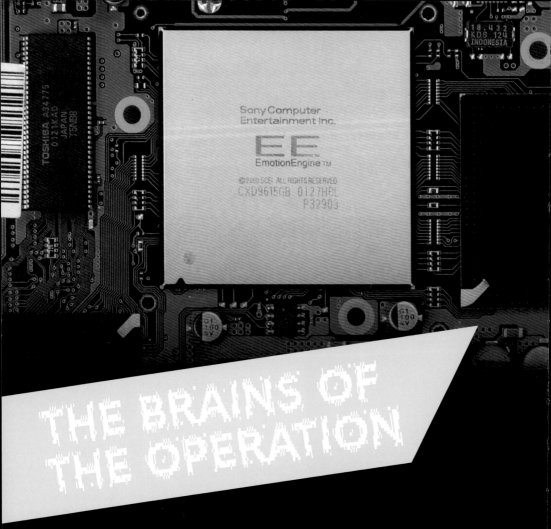

THE BRAINS OF THE OPERATION

Game consoles have to be able to think for themselves. Imagine you're playing a basketball video game and the other team is just standing around. Sure, it might be fun at first to run past them and leap into the air for a couple of slam dunks. But it would get boring pretty quickly. For the opposing players to fight back, we're going to need to give the console a brain. This brain is known as the central processing unit, or CPU for short.

Any kind of video game console or other computer needs a CPU. A console's CPU does three basic things. First, it performs math. Second, it makes decisions based on rules that the game creators gave it. And third, it moves information from one place to another.

The Wii U CPU has the power to send graphics and sound to two screens: one on the TV and one on the controller.

Let's go back to that basketball video game to check out examples of all three things. First, the math. When you shoot the ball, the console has to figure out where the ball goes. How far away from the basket were you? How hard was the shot? How good are the shooting skills of the player you're using? The CPU crunches all these numbers to decide how the ball flies through the air. The CPU also follows rules. Imagine you just hit the game-winning shot. The game creators have to give the CPU the following rule: the player with the higher score wins. Even basic stuff like that has to be spelled out for the CPU. Finally, the CPU moves information around. When you win the basketball game, confetti falls from the ceiling and a victory song plays. The CPU grabs the graphics and sound for these things and puts them onto the screen.

As you can probably tell, the CPU is the true brains of the operation when it comes to gaming. Without it, nothing would get done.

THE BRAINS OF THE BRAIN

CPUs contain amazingly tiny devices called transistors. The newest CPUs have more than a billion of them, each ten thousand times smaller than the width of a human hair. Each one simply switches on and off. By doing this in the right order, the transistors help the CPU do its three basic tasks.

A SOFTWARE KERNEL THAT REALLY POPS!

When you hear the word *kernel*, you probably think of the piece of corn that your microwave turns into popcorn. But it turns out that *kernel* is also a word for the core of any computer's software. And that includes the software inside video game consoles. Just be sure not to stick your PlayStation in a microwave.

software = any kind of computer program, including video games

The main job of the kernel is pretty simple. It helps the CPU talk to the software. Imagine the CPU is a sleek fighter jet and the software is the pilot. Without the pilot, the fighter jet is just sitting around the runway rusting its wings off. And without the jet, the pilot is just kicking rocks down the runway. Same thing with the CPU and the software. They're useless without each other. But when they come together, they become amazingly powerful. The kernel is what makes this teamwork possible.

But that's not all the kernel does. It also helps the software talk to the other important pieces of hardware besides the CPU. These include the memory and the controllers that make video games possible. In other words, no kernel, no game.

hardware = any kind of computer program, including video games

THE OPERATING ROOM

The kernel is the main part of what's known as the operating system, or OS. This is software that the computer uses to launch other programs, whether they're games, Internet browsers, or word processors. You might have heard about some of the operating systems on computers. Do Windows, Linux, or Mac OS ring any bells? Nearly all the world's computers run on one of these three operating systems.

The kernel is what lets the CPU talk to the joystick, the mouse, the keyboard, and any other hardware connected to a game console.

```
int size( ) const
{ return currentSize; }

object & operator[]( int index )

if( index < 0 || index >= currentSize
    throw ArrayIndexOutOfBounds( );

return objects[ index ];

)

object & operator[]( int index ) c
```

WRITING IN CODE

"If the player presses A, the character jumps. If the player presses B, he shoots a fireball. Here comes a bad guy! JUMP ON HIS HEAD!"

Unfortunately, game creators can't create their games by writing with regular words. Turns out, creating games is a lot more complicated than that. Games must be written in special languages known as programming codes. Here's an example of some programming code.

This code, written in a language called C, displays the words "Super Mario" on the screen:

```
#include < stdio.h>
void main()
{
    printf("\nSuper Mario\n");
}
```

Yikes. A bit tough to read, right? Why does programming code look so different from regular language? The reason is that the CPU is not really all that smart. You have to give it very careful instructions for it to do its job properly. A computer only speaks a specific language, and that language is called programming code. A programmer uses this code to give the computer detailed instructions. To make a game, a programmer has to write many thousands of lines of code.

The programming code tells the CPU everything about the game: who the characters are, what they look like, where they are, and how they move. The programmer also makes sure that everything runs smoothly all the way through the game. Any tiny mistake in the programming code and the game might stop working. Programmers don't want a herd of angry gamers stampeding down their door if they find a game-ending programming error on the final level.

Programmers spend long hours working on the programming code for games.

REVVING UP THE GAME ENGINE

Programming games is tough. Long hours, late nights, and tons of work go into writing all those lines of code. But think about it: lots of code might stay the same from game to game. If you're making a first-person game, chances are another programmer has already written some code you need. The basic instructions that tell the CPU how the character moves, what the enemies do, and how the levels are built are probably pretty similar. Why not just reuse those parts

first-person game = a game in which the player sees through the eyes of the character

and drop them into your game all at once? These chunks of common programming code are known as game engines.

By taking care of the simple stuff, the game engine lets the designers and programmers focus on the stuff that will make their game unique. Imagine a game engine is the engine of a car. If you don't have to create the car's engine from scratch every time, you can spend more time making the car more stylish, the steering more responsive, and the seats more comfortable. The same thing is true when it comes to game engines. Basically, they make the process of creating a game easier and cheaper.

The 2007 game *Crysis* used a game engine known as CryEngine to produce incredible graphics.

AN EXPENSIVE ENGINE

Although game engines can make the overall cost of a game cheaper, they usually cost money to use. The best ones can cost many thousands of dollars. Some game companies just make engines to sell to other game creators rather than making games themselves.

WHERE GAMES LIVE

Just like people, games have to live somewhere. If the kernel and the CPU are going to use the game's code, they need to know where to find it.

From the 1970s to the 1990s, the most common home for games was on cartridges. These are pieces of plastic that contained computer memory chips. The memory chips hold the programming code that makes up the games. Along one edge of the cartridge, metal connectors can be seen. When this edge is plugged into the console, these connectors let the cartridge and the console talk back and forth to each other.

For the earliest video games, cartridges worked great. They were pretty cheap, and they didn't need to hold much information. Graphics and sound were simple, so they didn't take up much space. Back then, space was measured in bytes. Cartridges for the Atari 2600 held 4 kilobytes—4,000 bytes.

But by the 1990s, games were getting a lot more complicated. Amazing graphics and high-quality sound took up more and more space each year. Cartridges were able to keep up for a little while, but soon games were getting too big too fast. Fitting games into cartridges was starting to feel like fitting elephants into your pockets. The Nintendo 64, the last console to use cartridges, could hold up to 64 megabytes—64 million bytes. But one of its competitors used a new storage technology that held more than ten times that much.

bytes = single pieces of information

The PlayStation's CDs gave video game developers tons more space for their games.

This new competitor was the PlayStation. It used compact discs, or CDs, to hold its games. CDs could hold 700 megabytes, far more than the old cartridges could. This huge amount of storage space was available because CDs work very differently from cartridges.

A CD is a type of optical disc. On optical discs, information is contained in a long line that begins on the edge and winds around and around toward the middle. The line is extremely narrow and amazingly long. If you stretched it out, it would go on for more than 3 miles (5 kilometers)! Along the line are microscopic holes known as pits. By measuring the pits and the gaps between them, the game console can read the information on the disc.

But it didn't take long for this incredible new technology to become out of date. Soon games were filling up three or four CDs. Fortunately, scientists invented a new kind of optical disc with even more storage space. These were called DVDs, or digital video discs. They hold more than six times as much as CDs. A few years later, even newer optical discs called Blu-ray Discs came out. They can hold a whopping ten times more than DVDs. Many movies are sold on DVD or Blu-ray Disc. But did you ever notice that they're the same size as CDs? How did they cram even more storage space onto the same size disc?

The answer is in the pits. On DVDs and Blu-ray Discs, the line of pits is narrower than on CDs. This means that the line of information is even longer, so more information can be stored. DVDs and Blu-ray Discs are used on modern consoles. The PlayStation 3 uses Blu-ray Discs, and the Xbox 360 uses DVDs.

LASER DISCS

How do game consoles read the lines of information on CDs, DVDs, and Blu-ray Discs? The answer: very narrow beams of light called lasers. Consoles spin the discs at amazing speeds while shooting a laser toward the lines of information. DVDs use red lasers, while Blu-ray Discs use thinner ones. Can you guess what color they are?

Disc-based game consoles use lasers to read the information stored on the discs.

The CPU has to deal with a ton of stuff at once. It's constantly handling graphics, sound, enemies, and the buttons the player presses. In other words, the CPU is a serious multitasker. But it can't manage this juggling act all by itself. It's got a partner known as RAM. By the way, that's random-access memory—not a male sheep!

The game console's random-access memory holds onto programming code that is needed right away. It pulls the information off the cartridge or disc and then passes it to the CPU whenever it's needed. This speeds up the game and prevents long loading times.

Games that have a lot happening on-screen, such as *Civilization V*, need plenty of RAM to run smoothly.

Not having RAM would lead to some very unfortunate gameplay. Imagine you're in the middle of the latest *Halo* game. You're playing as a super soldier sent to defeat an alien invasion. You dash across an open field toward a giant alien crab and press the button to pull out your giant laser, and . . . whoops. Your laser cannon is still loading from the game disc. CRUNCH. Congratulations—you've gone from super soldier to appetizer.

RAM makes sure this doesn't happen. It loads everything—characters, weapons, backgrounds, and everything else—smoothly so gameplay isn't interrupted.

These four chips hold the RAM for Sega's Dreamcast console.

FROM CONSOLE TO TV

Getting your game from the console to the TV sounds simple, right? Just plug the cord from the console into the back of the TV. But it takes some serious technology to make it all happen. It's even more impressive when you find out what came before.

The cable that goes from the console to the TV is known as the AV output, or audio-video output. Early consoles used RF, or radio frequency cables. That technology was pretty much from the 1800s, and it showed. Graphics were blurry and fuzzy, and sound was just plain bad. But the consoles at the time weren't powerful enough to perform better than that anyway.

Later consoles used composite cables. This type of cable usually had three ends that went into the TV—yellow, red, and white. The yellow one carried the picture, while red and white carried sound. The quality was a little better but still not great. By the year 2000, console graphics had gotten amazingly good, but composite cables were making them look amazingly bad.

Finally, in 2006, the PlayStation 3 took AV outputs to the next level with HDMI. Using HDMI, consoles send high-definition graphics and ultra-crisp sound through a single cable. The latest and greatest consoles, including the Xbox 360 and the Wii U, also use HDMI cables. At last, AV outputs have caught up with the raw power of today's game consoles.

HDMI = high-definition multimedia interface

HDMI cables helped PlayStation 3 games look better than any console games that came before.

PUSHING THE GAME'S BUTTONS

So you've got a great game running on your console. The graphics are awesome, and the sound is crystal clear. But guess what? If you can't control what's happening on-screen, all you're doing is watching a movie. To make this into a real video game, we need to figure out a way for the player to tell the game what to do. Enter the controller.

Practically every controller in gaming history has had one or more buttons. But how do they work? Think of each button as being a switch. Like a light switch, a button can be either "on" or "off." When you flick on a light switch, you're letting electricity flow through to the lightbulb, causing it to illuminate. Game controller buttons work the same way.

Imagine you're in the middle of an intense battle in a fighting game. You want your character to throw a knockout punch, so you hit the A button. When you press it, a tiny piece of metal in the A button touches another piece of metal inside the controller. Electricity flows between the two pieces and sends a signal back to the game console. The CPU figures out which button was pressed and checks the code instructions for what to do if the player hits A. The code tells the CPU to have your player swing his fist for the knockout. POW! Nice work. But really, the controller and the CPU did all the hard work.

Game companies had some seriously weird ideas for new controllers in the 1990s.

POSITION
6/6

HEALTH
99%
+0'03.50
TO RECORD

LAP
2/3

1ST WASHINGTON 0'18.0
2ND EMERSON +0'00.27
3RD F. ALOHEW +0'00.63
4TH T. WHITE +0'00.85
5TH C. CAVALL +0'01.50
6TH EUA +0'03.17

TAPPED OUT

Buttons are great for some games. And they were the only way to
play for many years. But nowadays, millions of players
are controlling their games in totally new
ways. If you've ever used an iPhone, a
Nintendo 3DS, or a Nintendo Wii U, you're
familiar with one of these new control
technologies. Can you guess what it is?
That's right: touch screens.

touch screens =
screens that you
can touch to
control rather than
using buttons

There are a few different types of touch screens. The technology
is super advanced but surprisingly easy to understand. The first
major type of screen uses resistive touch.

This is the kind used by the 3DS and the Wii U. These screens have two layers—plastic on top and glass below. When you tap the screen, the two layers touch. Electricity from the screen flows between them, sending a signal to the CPU that says where the tap happened. Resistive touch screens are very accurate, but they don't always respond quickly to touches.

The next cool touch tech is called capacitive touch. The iPhone and other smartphones use this kind of screen. Like the resistive touch screens, these have two layers. When you tap the screen, electricity from your screen goes into your finger. This CPU can tell how much electricity left the screen to find out where the screen was touched. Capacitive touch screens aren't quite as accurate as resistive ones, but they are super responsive. This responsiveness is part of what makes smartphone games like *Angry Birds* so popular.

The controller for the Nintendo Wii U console includes a built-in resistive touch screen.

A PLAYER IN MOTION

You turn on your game console and stand in front of your TV screen. Your hands are empty. There is no controller to be found. Suddenly, you move your hand. The on-screen menu follows your movement. Just a few years ago, this scene was a science fiction dream. But recently, games that use this type of control—known as motion control—are some of the most popular on the planet. You've probably had a chance to try playing a Wii, an Xbox Kinect, or a PlayStation Move. But how do these incredible new controls work?

The Wii and the Move use a different type of motion control than the Kinect. In these types, the player must still hold a controller. But make no mistake, these are no ordinary controllers. Looking a bit like TV remotes, they are packed with devices that can figure out where the controller is and how it moves. This information is sent back to the console. The result is that when you swing the controller like a sword, your character on-screen swings her sword too. When you hold it like a Ping-Pong paddle, you can knock the on-screen ball back to your opponent.

The Kinect is more like the sci-fi scenario from before. No controller is needed. The Kinect uses some seriously cool technology to pull this off. You put a small device next to the TV, and it shoots out thousands of infrared dots all across the room. The dots are normally invisible, but you can see them if you wear night vision goggles. The Kinect can tell how long it takes for the light from these dots to bounce back. Based on this, it can tell if there is a person in front of it and what that person is doing.

infrared = a type of light that is invisible to the naked eye

Gamers using the Xbox Kinect don't need to hold a controller.

BREAKTHROUGHS IN GAME TECHNOLOGY

Throughout the history of video games, some games took advantage of new advances in technology. The creators of these games had a great understanding of how games work. Not only that, but they knew how to transform this new technology into a fun experience for players. Here are five of these games. Each of them highlights a particular part of video game technology.

Controller: *Super Mario 64* (Nintendo 64, 1996)

Most games are designed with the console's controller in mind. But *Super Mario 64* might be the only game where the opposite is true. Nintendo mastermind Shigeru Miyamoto knew that the Nintendo 64's first game had to be amazing. So he designed the controller to work perfectly with the game. The result was that Mario's first 3D adventure had incredibly fluid controls. Earlier 3D platformer games had been clunky and hard to use. But the Nintendo 64's joystick let players control the portly plumber with ease.

Storage: *Final Fantasy VII* (PlayStation, 1997)

Square, the makers of the *Final Fantasy* series of role-playing games, originally planned to make *Final Fantasy VII* for the Super Nintendo. But they were concerned that the cartridges used on the Super Nintendo wouldn't have enough space for their epic game. When Nintendo announced that their next console, the Nintendo 64, would also use cartridges, Square decided they'd had enough. They made *Final Fantasy VII* for the PlayStation instead. The game ended up spanning three discs, and it became one of the most popular games in history.

RAM: *The Legend of Zelda: Majora's Mask* (Nintendo 64, 2000)
How do you follow the best game of all time? That was the challenge for *The Legend of Zelda: Majora's Mask*. It was the follow-up to *The Legend of Zelda: Ocarina of Time*, a game that many consider the best ever made. Finally, Nintendo figured out a way to top it. They would beef up the console itself. Along with the game, they introduced the Expansion Pak. Players could plug the Pak into the Nintendo 64 to double the console's RAM. The added memory allowed the game creators to make the game world larger and more detailed. Many gamers felt that *Majora's Mask* lived up to the previous game.

Engine: *Half-Life 2* (PC, 2004)
Half-Life 2 introduced Source, a new engine created by Valve Software. The engine featured advanced animation and lighting, creating stunning graphics. It also made it easy for gamers to play against one another online. The engine proved to be amazingly flexible. Although it was originally made for first-person shooter games, it was later used for practically every kind of game you can imagine. Almost ten years after it came out, it is still being used today.

Motion Control: *Wii Sports* (Nintendo Wii, 2006)
Wii Sports didn't feature amazing graphics or a stunning sound track. But it still became one of the most influential games of all time, all thanks to its innovative motion controls. The game came with Wii consoles, and it showed what the new system could do. Even people who didn't usually play games found *Wii Sports'* bowling, baseball, and tennis games crazy fun. Within a few years of the release of the Wii and *Wii Sports*, Nintendo's rivals Sony and Microsoft had both released their own motion controllers.

Atari 2600 Teardown
http://www.ifixit.com/Teardown/Atari-2600-Teardown/3541/1
The people at iFixit take apart all sorts of electronics to see what makes them tick. In this article, they take apart an Atari 2600—one of the earliest game consoles. If you want to check out what high-tech games looked like in the 1970s, take a look.

How Video Game Systems Work
http://www.howstuffworks.com/video-game.htm
Want more information about how game consoles work, including lots of technical details? Then this is the place for you.

Peckham, Matt. *Kinect Has a Thousand Eyes Viewed with Night Vision Goggles*
http://www.pcworld.com/article/209881/kinect_has_a_thousand_eyes
_viewed_with_night_vision_goggles.html
You probably don't have night vision goggles just lying around your house. But don't sweat it—someone on the Internet does. They've taken pictures and video of a Kinect in action. Check out how Kinect uses thousands of infrared dots to capture players' motions.

Source Engine
http://source.valvesoftware.com/
Valve Software's website features tons of information on their influential Source game engine. Learn about how it handles physics, graphics, and audio, among tons of other stuff. Boatloads of cool screenshots let you see how these things look in actual games.

Super Scratch Programming Adventure!: Learn to Program by Making Cool Games. San Francisco: No Starch Press, 2012.
Want to learn more about writing your own programming code? Check out this handy book, and you'll be making your own games in no time.

White, Ron, and Timothy Downs. *How Computers Work.* Indianapolis: Que Publishing, 2008.
A video game console is basically a computer that does one thing: run video games. So if you're craving more information about how all the parts of computers work, check this out. Tons of great pictures and illustrations make the info fun and easy to read.

Atari 2600, 5, 15
AV outputs, 20–21

Blu-ray Discs, 16–17

cartridges, 14–15, 16, 18, 28
CDs, 16–17
central processing unit, 6–7, 8–9,
    11, 12, 14, 18, 23, 25
controllers, 9, 22–23, 26–27, 28, 29

DVDs, 16–17

electricity, 22–23, 25

Final Fantasy VII, 28

game engines, 13

Half-Life 2, 29
hardware, 9

iPhone, 24–25

kernel, 5, 8–9, 14

motion controls, 26–27, 29

Nintendo 64, 15, 28, 29

operating systems, 9

PlayStation, 8, 16
PlayStation 3, 5, 17, 21
programmers, 11, 12–13
programming code, 10–11, 12–13,
    14, 18

random-access memory, 18–19, 29

software, 5, 8–9,
storage, 5, 15, 16–17, 28
Super Mario 64, 28

*The Legend of Zelda: Majora's
    Mask*, 29
touch screens, 24–25
transistors, 7

Wii, 26–27, 29
Wii Sports, 29
Wii U, 21, 24–25

Xbox Kinect, 26–27

PHOTO ACKNOWLEDGMENTS

The images in this book are used with the permission of: © Yoshikazu Tsuno/AFP/Getty Images, p. 4; Evan Amos, pp. 5, 6, 8 (left), 14, 16, 19 (bottom), 22; © Mark Lennihan/ AP Images, p. 7; © successo/Shutterstock Images, p. 8 (right); © imagebroker.net/ SuperStock, p. 9; © RapidEye/iStockphoto, p. 10; © Tom Landers/The Boston Globe/ Getty Images, p. 11; © Fabrice Dimier/Bloomberg/Getty Images, p. 12; © NVIDIA Corporation/PRNewsFoto/AP Images, p. 13; © Tsugufumi Matsumoto/AP Images, p. 15; © Hemera/Thinkstock, pp. 17, 26; © iStockphoto/Thinkstock, p. 18; © 2K Games/ Firaxis Games/AP Images, p. 19 (top); © vilax/Shutterstock Images, p. 20; © Sony Computer Entertainment/AP Images, p. 21; © Richard Drew/AP Images, p. 23; © pressureUA/iStockphoto, p. 24; © Barone Firenze/Shutterstock Images, p. 25; © Casey Rodgers/AP Images for Xbox, p. 27; © Kevork Djansezian/AP Images, p. 28; Red Line Editorial, p. 29.

Front cover: © Junko Kimura/Getty Images.

Main body text set in Calvert MT Std Regular 11/16.
Typeface provided by Monotype Typography.